GHOSTS IN THE HILLS

THE HISTORY AND HAUNTS OF QUAIL RUN RANCH

CYNTHIA ACKLEY NUNN

America Through Time is an imprint of Fonthill Media LLC
www.through-time.com
office@through-time.com

Published by Arcadia Publishing by arrangement with Fonthill Media LLC
For all general information, please contact Arcadia Publishing:
Telephone: 843-853-2070
Fax: 843-853-0044
E-mail: sales@arcadiapublishing.com
For customer service and orders:
Toll-Free 1-888-313-2665

www.arcadiapublishing.com

First published 2019

ISBN 978-1-63499-163-6

Typeset in 10pt on 13pt Sabon
Printed and bound in England

Contents

Dedication

In Memory of Angela Gibbons, who left us to fly to the angels on May 20, 2019

This book is dedicated to all those who joined me in my journey to research the history of Quail Run Ranch and to brave the rustic conditions we endured in efforts to record the rumored haunting. Colin Nunn, John Childress, Pattie Zadra Childress, Don Gibbons, Michael Hanna, Frank Lara, Cheryl Krause, Tim McCabe, Tammy McCabe, Aaron Deutsch, Mandy Briers & Joyce McCarthy, and Cody Logan–thank you!

Thanks are also owed to all our API team members who may not have been able to participate in person, but who provided support, input, unwavering encouragement, and research backup: Cheryl Natriello, Lisa Langsdorf Cloran, Scott Cloran, Jenna Lynn Hulette, Bobbi Goodman, Rae Clark, Sharon Biehl, Michael Aaron Kuntz, Stacey McAda Wright, Raymond "Badlizard" Rolón, Michelle Vella- Rolón, Cathy "Flip" Garziano, Howie Eury, Sharon Brentnall, Dara Tolson Eury, Kaitlyn Eury, Carolyn Lohr, Mary Jessica-Elaine Dodge, and Chris Hickerson.

Special thanks go to Brian Logan, without whom this would not have been possible. All photos are credited to the author unless otherwise stated.

Introduction

I grew up in the smallish town of Simi Valley, located in Southern California and just over the other side of the Los Angeles County line. As a child and teenager, I was an explorer and spent many happy hours hiking in the local hills and riding my bike over the Santa Susana Pass Road or Box Canyon to hang out in the Los Angeles County areas of Chatsworth and Canoga Park. Yet in all my years of wandering in search of new places, never did I come across Quail Run Ranch. I had never even heard of it and was unaware of its existence. We knew about and grew up with tales of the infamous Spahn Ranch, which we avoided out of fear that Charles Manson still held some supernatural power over the place, even from behind prison walls. Stories of weird cults with even weirder leaders who once populated our peaceful hills were also familiar. But Quail Run Ranch never hit our radar. I first heard about it from Brian Logan, caretaker of the ranch, while conducting a paranormal investigation of the old Pass Club on Santa Susana Pass Road. He asked if our team would like to check it out and conduct some investigations. Naturally, we said yes. We were too intrigued by the accounts he and others had to share with us to pass up the opportunity. We made our first preliminary visit during a hot summer afternoon. We were amazed. We were awestruck. We were hooked. The property, vacant since the last owner died, contained homes from three different eras, as well as numerous outbuildings and a pet cemetery. What followed were multiple investigations and lots of research into the history of this fascinating jewel forgotten in the hills of Southern California.

1

Early History

The ranch is located in a canyon with fairly rugged terrain, with the only access being rutted dirt roads with steep drops to the canyon floor below on either side. The drive to the location is not for the fainthearted or those who are afraid of heights.

This area is rich in history, stretching all the way back to about 6500 B.C.E., when the Tongva/Kizh people probably first settled the cave-filled canyons, using both the sandstone shelters as homes and willow huts. They inhabited roughly 4,000 square miles of land in California, and at the time of European contact had a population of between 5,000 and 10,000. Today, only 1,700 claim full or partial Tongva ancestry. They are related to the Chumash people who also lived in this area.

In the 1500s, the Tongva people had limited, brief contact with the Spaniards marching through the area in their unceasing search for gold and other resources to exploit. It wasn't until after 1770 that these native peoples had any sustained contact with Europeans, which would end up having a mostly negative impact on their way of life and culture.

This area, along with many other acres of land, became the property of the San Fernando Mission, under the control of Franciscan priests, who treated the native population as slave labor. Once a native was baptized, they could be held against their will and forced to live at the mission. Soldiers were stationed at the mission and were used to prevent anyone from escaping. Attempts to escape brought severe corporal punishment.

Remnants of the Tongva people can still be found at the ranch in the form of petroglyphs, pictographs, grinding stones, and the caves they lived or sheltered in.

Chumash pictographs in Simi Valley dating to 500 CE.
[By Niceley, Own work, CC BY-SA 3.0, https://commons.wikimedia.org/w/index.php?curid=35222869]

A lava rock grindstone.

Another view of the lava rock grindstone. The question is whether or not this was actually used by the Tongva People. The father of the last owner of the property made a name for himself for carving grindstones from lava rock and then selling them.

This is an authentic grindstone used by the Tongva People, who often carved multiple grinding holes in a single large rock or boulder.

Full view of the authentic grindstone.

Another view of the authentic grindstone.

This would have been the perfect spot to watch for the arrival of anyone approaching the area.

The caves in these sandstone rock formations offered welcome relief from the harsh sun.

More caves dotted throughout the sandstone formations.

2

Rancho Ex-Mission San Fernando

Between 1845 and 1846, the Mission began to release its stranglehold on some of the lands and allowed secularization. In 1845, Odón, Urbano, and Manuel, three men of the Chumash People, petitioned Governor Pio Pico for close to 9,000 acres of land. Governor Pico only granted about 2,250 acres. The Second Alcalde (mayor) of Los Angeles, Juan Sepulveda, then came in and surveyed off a parcel that was roughly only 1,125 acres. Although Odón and Urbano accepted this short-changing of the parcels they were granted, they spent many years, as late as to 1870, legally disputing the boundaries. But this didn't stop them from using the original 9,000 acres at various times.

Our area of interest came to be known as El Escorpion de las Salinas and was occupied by Chief Odón's daughter, Maria Dolores Odón, and her husband, Pierre Domec, a Frenchman who arrived in Los Angeles in 1844 at the age of twenty-four.

Left: Maria Dolores Odón and husband Pierre Domec. *[Photo credit Leonis Adobe Archives]*

Below: These formations would have been a familiar sight to Maria and Pierre.

Another familiar site to Pierre and Maria would have been this hill formation with caves located at the top and around the other side.

More of the land and sandstone formations on the area known as El Escorpion de las Salinas.

3

ANNA SWAIN GALLOW

The Domec property was eventually parceled out and sold to homesteaders in the early 1900s. Our property of interest was homesteaded by a woman named Anna T. Gallow, also known as Annie, who was living apart from her husband for many years. She purchased this parcel in 1911 and built her small homestead, as required by government homesteading laws.

Annie's small original homestead is still standing on the property and is now referred to as the Chapel, for reasons that will become obvious in the photos. Records on Annie are scarce, but we do know that this building would have been erected no later than the year 1912.

The homestead consisted of a small living space downstairs, with just enough room for a table, a few chairs, maybe a writing desk, the wood burning stove, and a rudimentary kitchen. Annie's bedroom was a small loft room upstairs accessed by a ladder.

Over the years, a small indoor bathroom was added on containing a toilet, sink and shower, a closet built in to the loft, a porch constructed on to the outside of the house, and exquisitely carved small wooden cupboards installed in the tiny kitchen area.

The homestead now stands as a huge piece of folk art in its own right due to the modifications it contains. What we know is that these modifications were done by at least one, if not two men, from a local family of master masons, woodworkers, and artisans. We just don't know when, but newspaper accounts gave us some clues that these updates happened around 1919. It is the author's belief that Frank Knapp, Sr. carried out the renovations for Annie while she still lived at the property, and later his son, Joseph, carried on with what his father had started. This could explain why Joseph Knapp later purchased this property.

Annie was born in Smith, Mahoning County, Ohio, *circa* 1850/51 to John Swain, born in New Jersey in 1819, and her mother, Mary Ann Chance, who was born in Ohio. Annie's full real name at birth was Ann Athalia Swain. She had two sisters, Zalia and Sarah, who married Frederick C. Barrows.

Anna and her family were in Wright Territory, Minnesota, by 1860. Living nearby was Joseph Gallow, her future husband. By 1870, Annie and Joseph M. Gallow were married and living in Monticello, Minnesota. Annie and her family lived only about ninety minutes away from Laura Ingalls Wilder. Future census records show that Annie and Joseph must have had a less than ideal marriage, because we find Annie living with her father while Joseph resided elsewhere. An interesting note is that Joseph and Annie are shown as living together as man and wife in 1870 and 1880, but according to vital records, they were not legally married until October 15, 1886, in Freeborn, Minnesota. In any case, by 1889, they had permanently separated.

After Annie's father passed away in 1905, she packed up and moved to the state of Washington, where she operated a dressmaking parlor in Aberdeen.

A news item from the Aberdeen Herald, November 26, 1906, states:

> **NEW DRESSMAKING PARLORS**
>
> Mrs. Annie Gallow and Miss Blanche Albright have opened dressmaking parlors in Room 17, Dabney block (over Red Cross Pharmacy). Mrs. Gallow is just from the East, and is prepared to do strictly up-to-date, first-class work, and will be pleased to have you call, inspect models, and get estimates on any style garment you may select.

In 1907, she visited her sister in California, according to a *Los Angeles Times* news item, August 18, 1907, which states:

> Mrs. Z. L. Bathbrick of Palmer Avenue is entertaining her sister, Mrs. Annie Gallow and Miss Blanche Albright of Aberdeen, Washington.

Note: The sister was named Zalia L.Bathrick and Blanche Albright was a cousin. Zalia and her husband Jefferson had two sons, Charles & Floyd and a daughter named Margaret.

By 1910, according to the census, Annie was living in Long Beach, CA. Her husband, Joseph, listing himself as "widowed," was living in the Veteran's Home in Yount Township, Napa, CA, where he died in 1930. Annie didn't stay in Long Beach very long, as we find that by 1911 she had purchased her homestead claim, and by 1912 she was running the Owensmouth Café, the first restaurant in that area. The specialty was the much-loved chicken pie. It was reported that on December 12, 1912, Anna served over 100 people in her restaurant. She sold the cafe to J. Detrow in 1916.

We have some local news accounts about the ranch during the time Annie lived there. The January 23, 1916, issue of the *Los Angeles Times* states:

> Mrs. Anna L. Gallow arrived from her ranch home near Owensmouth Tuesday and will spend several weeks with her sister, Mrs. Zella L. Bathrick, of West Palmer Avenue.

On November 27, 1916, Annie was officially granted free and clear ownership of her property. A certificate was issued stating, "The claim of Annie T. Gallow has been established and duly consummated, in conformity to the Law."

The December 22, 1916, edition of the *Owensmouth Gazette* reported: "Mrs. A. T. Gallow had as guests at her mountain ranch on Sunday Mr. & Mrs. Watson of Burbank, Mr. & Mrs. Ingram of Tropico, Mrs. Echels of New York."

The January 12, 1917, issue of the *Owensmouth Gazette* announced:

> Miss Rooksby chaperoned a party of young people on a hike to Mrs. Gallow's mountain home on Saturday (Jan. 6th). The day was ideal and all enjoyed the trip very much. The members of the party were Jessie Becksted, Gladys Riddle, Lenore Cravens, Elizabeth Delaway, Earl & Lloyd Carder, Beem Hyden.

It is the March 9, 1917, edition of the *Owensmouth Gazette* that provides us with a real gift, as it reveals the original name that Annie gave to her ranch, the romantic but apt title of "the Eyrie," as shown in the quote below.

> Mrs. Gallow invites all the people of Owensmouth and vicinity to join in a picnic at her mountain home, the Eyrie, on Saturday, March 10. Arrangements will be made to have wagons at the foot of the mountain to carry those who are unable to walk up the trail.

On February 21, 1919, it was reported that Anna was ill due to lameness. However, she soon recovered, and on July 25, 1919, the *Owensmouth Gazette* reported that Annie was contemplating extensive improvements on her place near Owensmouth. We can safely assume that she was talking about the ranch, which was considered "near Owensmouth." We believe this is when Frank Knapp, Sr., father of future owner, Joseph, carried out the artistic improvements on Annie's homestead, the Eyrie. On August 15, 1919, the *Owensmouth Gazette* announced that she was taking bids from contractors to build a road to her "mountain home."

On August 29, 1919, Anna received a visitor to the Eyrie, nephew Frank Barrows, who drove down from Antioch, California, in his auto. Frank, a married man with children and a music teacher, would be arrested in 1936 and sent to San Quentin Prison for "morals charges" committed against young boys. He pleaded guilty by reason of insanity, but was still found guilty. He spent five years in San Quentin. Frank may have viewed Anna as a mother figure as he is shown in records as living with Joseph and Anna at least twice in his early years, once at sometime between birth and age two years, as his mother died during his birth, and again at the age of eight years. As Anna and her husband had never had children, she may also have viewed Frank as a surrogate son.

Annie, very much an integral part of the larger Owensmouth/Canoga Park community, was involved in many local events and activities. Annie, a member of the local Red Cross, was also considered a qualified legal adviser and helped register people to vote. She was also the librarian at the Owensmouth Library, with a news article mentioning that she was the most competent librarian they had ever had to date. In 1918, Anna was head of the Liberty Bonds committee for her area, and she also was noted as having sewn a new service flag. In 1919, she ran a flower sale to help the library purchase more furniture. In September 1924, the town of Owensmouth's American Legion Post dedicated its new clubhouse. Annie, along with Miss Anna Hunt, presented the service flag.

In March 1925, Annie hosted a luncheon for Foster Kreis, member of the American consulate in Shanghai, China. He was in the area visiting his parents, Mr. & Mrs. Charles Kreis of Minnesota. Also attending the luncheon were Mrs. Nannie Cameford of Minnesota, Mrs. Newell Irving of Bell, California, Mrs. Mary Pratt of Hollywood, Mrs. Cora Kreis of Inglewood, and Mrs. Elsa Kearns of Los Angeles.

In 1930, Annie witnessed Owensmouth officially being renamed Canoga, which apparently was the original name of the area at one time. During this time, Annie's cousin, Blanche Albright, was living with her.

Annie died on December 19, 1939, in Los Angeles County. When she passed away, the parcel was purchased by its last owner, Joseph Knapp.

Los Angeles 017275

4—1003-R.

The United States of America,

To all to whom these presents shall come, Greeting:

WHEREAS, a Certificate of the Register of the Land Office at **Los Angeles, California,** has been deposited in the General Land Office, whereby it appears that, pursuant to the Act of Congress of May 20, 1862, "To Secure Homesteads to Actual Settlers on the Public Domain," and the acts supplemental thereto, the claim of **Annie T. Gallow** has been established and duly consummated, in conformity to law, for the **Lots one and two of Section twenty-eight in Township two north of Range seventeen west of the San Bernardino Meridian, California, containing ninety-three and eighty-eight-hundredths acres,**

Anna Gallow's Approved Land Grant. *[General Land Office archives, Los Angeles, CA]*

Path leading to Annie's homestead, also known originally as the Eyrie, and now as the Chapel.

The old gate leading to Annie's homestead.

Distant view of Annie's homestead, the Eyrie.

Above: Closer view of Annie's homestead.

Left: North facing wall of the homestead, making it clear why this is now referred to as the Chapel House. The author believes the brick and rock work were added between 1919 and 1920, by local master mason and craftsman Frank Knapp, Sr. The work is very much his typical style and each rock and brick would have been hard carved or molded by him. Frank, Sr. specialized in religious art, which many think is due to the rumor that he was a defrocked Catholic priest.

Right: Straight-on view of the Chapel House brick and rock work.

Below. Another view of the Chapel House brick and rock work

View of the Chapel House brick and rock work and a peek at the window addition and some of the hand carved beam work.

A close-up of the cross, which appears to have had a carving of Jesus on it at one time. Some of the arch brickwork appears to be carved from local lava rocks.

East view of the homestead showing the 1919 or 1920 addition of the loft dormer windows.

Another view of the East side of the homestead showing the 1919 or 1920 addition of the small bathroom.

Left: Close-up of the North (Chapel) side of the homestead. The beams and Swiss style roof were probably part of the 1919/1920 renovations. The stove pipe is the original from 1911.

Below: Upward view of the underside of the roof section.

Another view of the beams, which at one time had intricate carvings.

Michael Hanna and Brian Logan inspecting the south side of the house.

A view of the small succulent garden near the second path leading to the homestead house.

Another view of the east side of the house, where it looks like another covered patio may have existed.

The covered patio over the entrance door to the homestead. The author believes that the carved wood posts and the side wall, along with the flagstone patio, were the work of Frank Knapp, Sr., and the more modern patio cover the work of his son Joseph.

Close-up of the carved patio posts.

An outside table or altar at the Homestead House. The work could have been done by Joseph Knapp, but most likely it was done by his father, Frank.

Another view of the altar table. The bricks used to create a small patio in front of the altar are stamped with the mark of FLINT SM. These were manufactured by Gladding, McBean and Co. in Alberhill, Riverside County, California, and were made between the years 1926 to 1935. This makes it more probable that Frank Knapp, Sr. did this work.

Another view of the small garden leading up one of the paths to the Homestead House.

An artistic compilation of painted metal plates.

An artistic compilation of painted metal plates hanging on south wall of Homestead House.

One of the old propane tanks used to help power the Homestead House.

Right: The entrance door to the Homestead House, hand carved by Frank Knapp, Sr.

Below: Intricately carved miniature cupboards, probably the work of Frank Knapp, Sr., hang above the small kitchen area of the Homestead House.

Side view of the miniature cupboards.

Another view of the miniature cupboards.

Original hand-painted tiles line the wall where the wood-burning stove used to sit in the Homestead House.

Another view of the tiled wall.

Handcrafted ladder leading up to the loft bedroom in the Homestead House.

Another view of the handcrafted loft ladder. In this image you can see the small closet built and hand carved by Frank Knapp, Sr.

John Childress sits atop the loft ladder.

Detail of the decorative carving on the underside of the loft closet.

Detail of the carved flower on the side of the loft closet.

One of the skillfully hand carved beams inside the Homestead House.

The inside of the dormer window in the loft, complete with built-in shelving.

Above left: View inside the small bathroom of the Homestead House.

Above right: The hand carved toilet inside the Homestead House.

4

The Hacienda House

We have no definite date for when the Hacienda House was built, but can make a pretty good estimate. In the 1920s, this property was actually enumerated in the census records for Simi Valley/Santa Susana. At that time, a company called the Southern California Investment Corporation of Los Angeles was building small, rustic cabins in the area for those wishing to escape the city. The style of the Hacienda House, and its situation at the head of a steep set of steps going up a hill, is very similar to the homes being built in the Santa Susana area. It is possible that Anna had it built by this company either for herself or to use as an investment property for weekend vacationers.

The interior of the house is largely inaccessible due to a fire in the recent past and all of the trash and debris piled up inside. There is also evidence of local wildlife nesting in it, as indicated by all of the droppings.

The house consists of a reasonable sized living room, one very small bedroom, a tiny bathroom, and an equally tiny kitchen. There is no evidence of a built-in fireplace, and the chimney outside appears to be strictly ornamental in nature.

What was odd is that the closet was filled with only men's clothing, of a style that Joseph Knapp seemed to favor. Since the Knapp house had only a single bed, there is a possibility that Joseph was actually living in this house. Obviously anything owned by Anna Gallow, the original owner of the Hacienda House, is no longer evident here. The stamp of Joseph is to be found all over, from the hand-built tables and patio chairs to the clothes in the closet.

Also located at this house is what we refer to as the Mystery Building. It could have been for food storage, but then again it could have been used for something that we would never even think of.

Next to the house is a Swiss or Austrian-style building that may have been a work shed of some sort for Joseph Knapp as it appears to be more modern than Anna Gallow's time. This building was also inaccessible due to all of the old furniture and other items stored in it.

Path leading to the arch and the Hacienda House.

Another view of the path leading to the arch and the Hacienda House.

API Team members examine and photograph the arch.

A view of the entire arch. The highly skilled craftsmanship marks this out as probably another example of Frank Knapp, Sr's work.

The other side of the arch. The area to the west of the arch was a large orchard at one time where a number of fruit varieties were grown. There was also a grape vineyard.

Close-up of the arch and wild succulents growing in front of it.

Close-up of the lamp hanging on the arch.

An original gate leaning against the arch. At one time, it was connected to the arch along with other gates now missing.

Right: A stone with fossils embedded in to the wall. It is not known if this is an actual collection of fossils or something created and carved by Frank Knapp, Sr. Another of the family properties, located in the Angeles National Forest, contains a similar fossil feature in a wall.

Below: The Hacienda House. Areas of the house's original walls and foundations are visible in places, and give us clues that lead us to believe it was built between the years of 1924 to 1935.

Above: A non-functioning chimney added on to the house and purely decorative. There is no fireplace inside the house.

Left: A close-up detail of decorative carving embedded in chimney.

View of the Hacienda House from the road.

Front porch of the Hacienda in black & white.

Front porch of the Hacienda in color.

Side view of Hacienda showing back patio and brickwork arch.

Arch to the back patio and kitchen entrance of the Hacienda.

Another shot of the arch to the back patio and kitchen entrance of the Hacienda.

Exterior side wall of the Hacienda kitchen.

On another visit we found that some of the kitchen's exterior wall boards had been removed to expose a dead bee colony.

Another shot of the dead bee colony in the exterior kitchen wall.

View inside one of the Hacienda house windows, which has been badly damaged by fire.

View inside another of the Hacienda house windows.

Inside the Hacienda. Access was limited due to the piled-up furniture, trash, and damage from a past fire.

Front door into the Hacienda.

Access stairs to the Hacienda from the lower path.

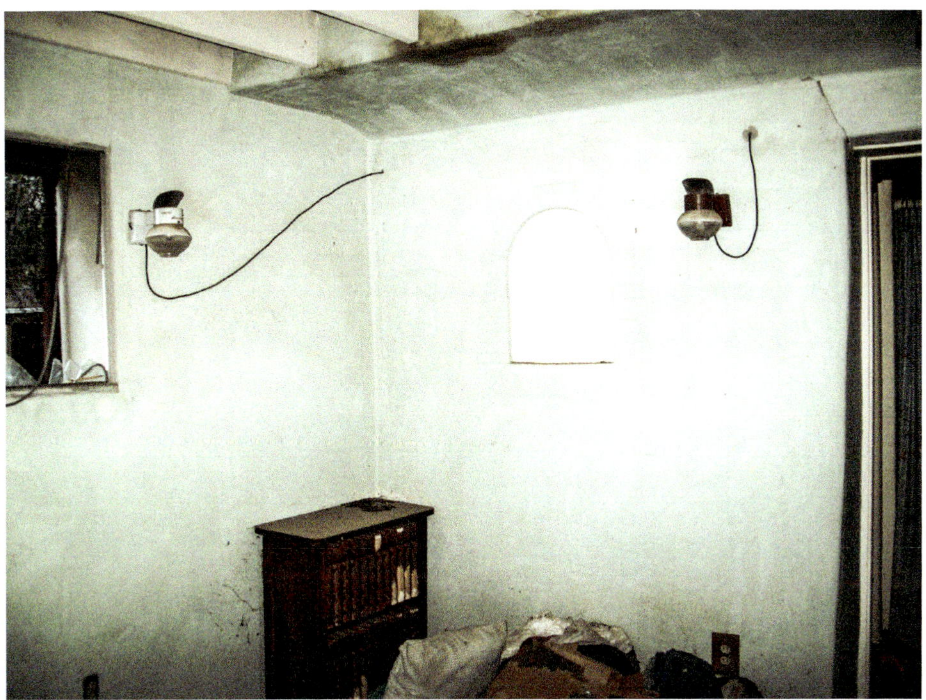

The living room of the Hacienda.

Side view of the Hacienda house and the small building that may have been used as some form of food storage.

Door to the mystery building.

Inside the mystery building.

Tower on top of the mystery building.

Another view of the tower on top of the mystery building.

Opposite above: Another closer view of the Tower on top of the mystery building.

Opposite below: The Swiss Chalet style building next to the Hacienda. We have no idea of what its original use was, but now it is full of old furniture and junk.

5

THE KNAPP HOUSE

After Anna Gallow died in 1939, the property was purchased by Joseph Knapp. It is possible that he wanted it due to his father Frank's mark and craftsmanship being found greatly in existence here. Like his father, Joseph was also a mason and craftsman. The Knapp house was hand built by Joseph in 1940.

Joseph Lincoln Knapp was born February 12, 1914, in Los Angeles, California, a son of Frank Knapp & Maria Johanna Meixer, who were both born in the Tyrol region of Austria. There has been a strong legend with some members of the family that Frank Knapp, Sr. had been a priest with the Catholic Church in Austria, but was defrocked for having an illicit affair with a nun. The author has not been able to find out if this is true or not. What we do know is that Frank, Sr. married, and he, along with his wife and three of Joseph's older siblings, immigrated to the United States sometime between 1902 and 1904, with evidence that Frank, Sr. came ahead, settled briefly in Pennsylvania, and then eventually moved the family to Owensmouth, California, about 1910.

Joseph Knapp had been married once in his life, to Ida Elenor Smith, daughter of Harvey Sylvester Smith & Soledad Catarina "Sallie" Sepulveda. They are listed in the 1940 census as living on Chatsworth Annex, Simi Valley/Santa Susana. That would be "Quail Run Ranch." The marriage was not a happy one and Ida soon left to move back in with her parents. About 1974, Virginia Maroney moved to the property as Joseph's common-law wife. Ida died on December 27, 1999. She is buried in Oakwood. Apparently they never divorced, which explains why Joseph and Virginia never married. It appears that Joseph and Ida may have had a son named Joseph L. Knapp II, but this is only speculation. All three, Joseph, Ida and Virginia, were devout Catholics. This makes one wonder how Joseph and Virginia dealt with living together as an unmarried couple, with things further complicated by the stigma of being adulterers since Joseph was still married. Just looking around the property and at the items left behind after the deaths of Joseph and Virginia, one can see that both were indeed still devout Catholics.

Joseph died June 2, 1991, in Santa Barbara, CA, at seventy-seven years old. He is buried in Oakwood Cemetery on Lassen St, near his parents. His headstone says:

> Always in Our Hearts
> Joe Knapp
> A Man of Courage
> June 2nd, 1991

The last owner of the property, by inheritance or prior agreement with family members of Joseph, was Virginia Elizabeth Maroney, girlfriend/common-law wife of Joseph Knapp. As mentioned earlier, she moved into the house sometime around 1974.

Virginia was born July 24, 1916, in Los Angeles, California, so she was just five months short of her 100th birthday when she passed away on February 11, 2016.

Her father was John George Maroney, born in Peytona, West Virginia, January 29, 1878. No information about who her mother was has been found.

There is very little information to be found about Virginia. One person who knew her, who wishes to remain anonymous, states that Virginia was an alcoholic, which at times caused distress to Joseph. Maybe this is why he ended up living in the Hacienda House, and then ultimately moving to Santa Barbara for the last year or so of his life.

We do know that both Joseph and Virginia were animal lovers and there is a pet cemetery next to the house containing the remains of their favorite dog and horse.

A photo of Joseph Knapp, builder of the Knapp House.

A photo of Joseph Knapp, on the right, with brother Frank, Jr. Joseph's brother Frank owned the Knapp Ranch in the Angeles National Forest. At one time, Frank partnered with King Gillette in attempts to find the Lost Padre Gold Mine. When Frank died in 1988 brother Joseph inherited the ranch in the Angeles National Forest, making him the owner of two ranches. *[photo credit from the album of Donna Bostick]*

Frank "Franz" Knapp, Sr., father of Joseph, photo taken in Austria. Frank, Sr. was from Tyrol and is wearing Tyrolean clothing typical of that era. *[Photographer unknown]*

The Joseph Knapp home, built by hand in 1940.

Another view of the Joseph Knapp home.

Joseph Knapp home in black & white.

Side view of the Joseph Knapp home. Living room and bedroom windows face out.

A storage hut behind the Knapp house, built by Joseph Knapp.

A green house or conservatory built by Joseph Knapp. We were unable to open the door and access due to over-growth.

Author isn't sure if this is a bread oven or a small brick oven, but feels that it was most likely created by Frank Knapp, Sr. In the distance is the Guardian Dog in the pet cemetery.

Hand carved miniature California Mission. It was most likely created by Frank Knapp, Sr., as he was making and selling these to customers in the late 1920s to 1930s. It is said in a news article that he carved miniature representations of every California Mission.

The Guardian Dog sits atop the burial location of the dog owned by Joseph Knapp. The dog was the companion of the horse Joseph owned, and the grave of the horse is located under the cross and headstone. It is not surprising that people working here have reported the sounds of a horse walking around.

A baptismal font carved by Frank Knapp, Sr.

Inside the small living room of the Knapp house. The chair belonged to Virginia Maroney, common-law wife of Joseph Knapp. She died in the house in 2016. The chair was probably here when Joseph was still alive.

Rocking chair in the Knapp living room.

The sofa and electric fireplace in the living room, with entrance to the kitchen.

The bed of Virginia Maroney, where she died. Everything was left like a time capsule.

The dresser in the small, single bedroom.

The kitchen of the Knapp house.

View of the ironing board extended from its storage cupboard.

The original wooden ironing board, as crafted and installed by Joseph Knapp in 1940. It is still in perfect working condition. This is just one of many charming original features of this house.

Kitchen door leading to the small enclosed back patio, where the API team found the strange little poppet or magic doll offering.

6

The Hauntings

After investigating another location claimed to be haunted, Brian Logan, the caretaker of the ranch, asked if we would like to investigate the property. Many people over the years have claimed to have seen paranormal activity at the ranch, some of which was quite unsettling and downright frightening. Multiple witnesses, mostly tough-as-nails construction workers, have seen the floating shadow figure of an apparition dressed in a long, gray, hooded cloak moving quickly through one of the fields on the property. These same witnesses refuse to stay on the property once the sun goes down. We have a drawing of this apparition provided by one of the witnesses, and the other witnesses concur with it. This figure has come to be known as the Tall Monk.

We ended up conducting three separate investigations at this location, including an overnight. For the overnight, only a few of us intended to stay all night at the property in haunted locations, but an unexpected storm rolled in, washing out the dirt road and forcing some members to stay. They preferred to stay in their vehicles and not in any of the buildings.

We collected many photos, as well as EVP recordings of our investigations, and team members witnessed or experienced incidents that we could not explain away, even after thorough attempts to do so. The ranch is a wonderful place trapped in time, but when the sun goes down, it truly is a different place. For the most part, the spirits who linger seem to be benign and friendly, with a few exceptions. Unfortunately, the scope of this book is limited, so sharing all reports would be impossible. However, more information will be shared on my author's blog, and to listen to some of the EVPs, I have set up a YouTube channel for you to visit and indulge your curiosity.

https://www.youtube.com/playlist?list=PLMPEsw4jZzD8abDeu_DiFVoUJoWSjv4Y8

Above: The strange object left in front of the door leading to the kitchen door entrance, found when we arrived to start our first investigation. It appeared to be some sort of poppet or offering. The team members chose to believe it was some sort of blessing and not a curse. *[photo credit John Childress]*

Left: Rocking chair in the living room of the Knapp house, with photo of Joseph for a trigger object to see if it would attract communication from him.

Right: One of our video cameras set to run in the kitchen/dining room area of Knapp house while the team members investigated other locations on the property.

Below: Recording equipment set up in the kitchen of the Knapp house.

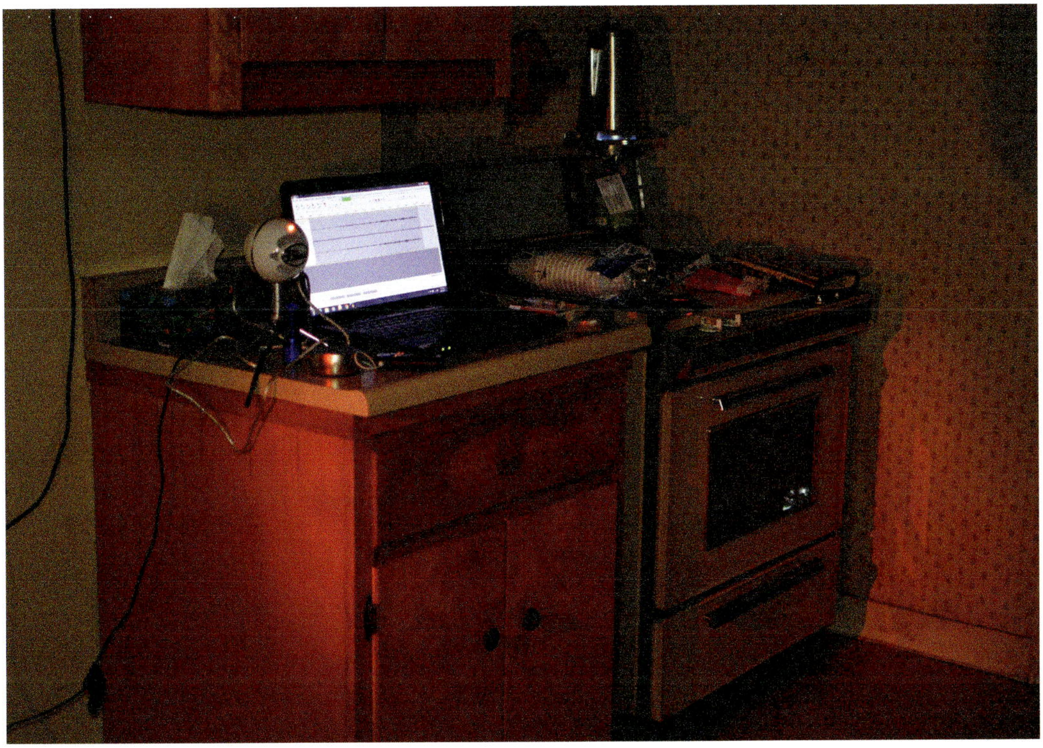

Above: Beds set up in the Knapp house living room for our third investigation, an overnight sleepover.

Left: Team members Colin Nunn and Mandy Briers on a break in between investigation sessions of the ranch.

Team member Don Gibbons.

Team member Aaron Deutsch.

Above: Team members Frank Lara and Mandy Briers on the patio of Knapp house.

Left: Team member Michael Hanna.

Team member Don Gibbons holds a vigil in the bedroom at Knapp house.

Michael Hanna, team psychic, at the arch leading to the Hacienda house. During this incident, the orbs in the two photos were not visible to the naked eye. Michael was sensing two spirits and asked them to come closer. The orbs were captured while the author was taking photos of Michael at that time.

Team member Tim McCabe on the path to the Hacienda house.

Team members Aaron Deutsch, Mandy Briers, Tim McCabe and Michael Hanna investigate the Hacienda house.

Colin Nunn and Michael Hanna inside the Homestead House, aka The Chapel, during the investigation. *[photo credit John Childress]*

Kitchen area of the Homestead, shot by the author from the top of the loft ladder.

Guest investigator Cody Logan investigating inside the Homestead house.

Night shot of the outside of the Homestead house taken by the author during investigation. Cody Logan is on the porch near the front door.

Interesting light anomaly captured by the author outside of the Homestead house. We have no idea what it is.

Drawing of the Tall Monk ghost as witnessed by Brian Logan and numerous construction workers who were at the property. *[Drawing produced by Brian Logan, reprinted with his permission.]*

Cody Logan and team member John Childress in the field where the Tall Monk figure is often seen.

While in the field where the Tall Monk is seen, team members John Childress, Cindy Nunn (the author), Cody Logan, and another male guest who did not want to be named, saw what looked like a huge shadowy black figure coming towards them. The author took a quick photo and then everyone started to walk backward slowly away from the figure. The male guest, a construction worker, having witnessed the figure in the past, became afraid and quickly left. Cody stopped and we could all see the shadowy figure in front of him. The author took another photo. Upon viewing later the orbs seen in the photos were spotted.

Photos taken in the field by team member John Childress just as we heard growls in the area. *[photo credit John Childress]*

Team member Michael Hanna in the backyard of Knapp house.

The author took this photo of the conservatory/greenhouse without flash and without any light source. The light coming from inside remains a mystery, but was captured at a time when Michael Hanna was sensing a female presence.

Three images captured consecutively by the author of the side patio at Knapp house. The white misty image in center photo is unexplained.

Strange light patterns captured by team member John Childress in the Knapp house living room. No flash was used and there was no light source. There is also a strange mist to the left. *[photo credit John Childress]*

Large orb captured over Virginia's chair at the time team member was asking her to make her presence known. *[photo credit John Childress]*

Team member Mandy Briers, happy we made it through a truly dark and stormy night at what we call Ghost Ranch, where we slept in the Joseph Knapp house.

58984

Frank Barrows

288a P.C. – Orange –
0 to 15 – Minn – 63 –
Musician – 5'5" –
Rud – Grey – Grey –
201 – Rec'd 5/11-36.
Paroled 6-5-41
Disch. from Parole 1/4/44

9 R 17
18 aR 16

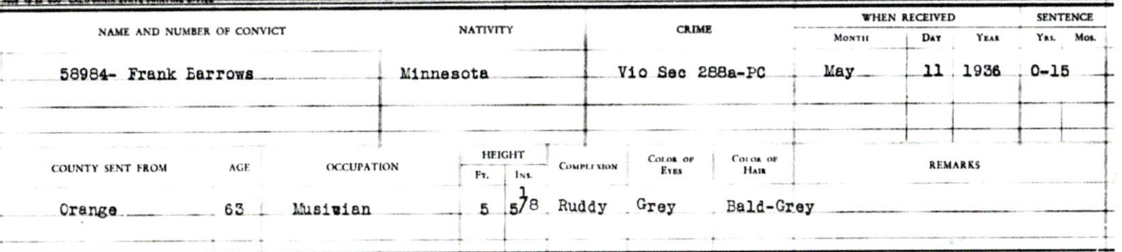

332

REGISTER AND DESCRIPTIVE LIST OF CONVICTS UNDER SENTENCE OF IMPRISONMENT IN THE STATE PRISONS OF CALIFORNIA

NAME AND NUMBER OF CONVICT	NATIVITY	CRIME	WHEN RECEIVED			SENTENCE	
			MONTH	DAY	YEAR	YRS.	MOS.
58984- Frank Barrows	Minnesota	Vio Sec 288a-PC	May	11	1936	0-15	

COUNTY SENT FROM	AGE	OCCUPATION	HEIGHT FT.	HEIGHT INS.	COMPLEXION	COLOR OF EYES	COLOR OF HAIR	REMARKS
Orange	63	Musivian	5	5 7/8	Ruddy	Grey	Bald-Grey	

San Quentin Prison register for Frank Barrows, nephew of Anna Gallow. During one of the investigations, we had all been confused by team psychic Michael Hanna picking up on a bad man who harmed children. As far as the records showed, no children had lived at this property. We thought maybe some farmhands or other workers had brought their children here. When this record of Frank Barrows came up as being a child molester, and the newspaper's mention of him visiting, the author was able to research and found his close relationship with Anna Gallow. *[Photo credit Department of Corrections. San Quentin State Prison Records, 1850–1950. ID #R135, California State Archives, Office of the Secretary of State, Sacramento, California.]*

Final Note

As curious as some of you may be, we request that you do not look for the property, or if you find it, do not trespass. It is actually well guarded by a singular of wild boars, descendants of the first ones from the area. They wander the property and will attack the wary.

The property was put up for sale and our biggest worry was that a developer would purchase it and tear down all of the historic buildings and the folk art of Frank Knapp, Sr. The author is happy to say that she was recently informed that the property has been purchased by a family who plan to make the houses livable again and they will be residing at the property and protecting its legacy.

Please respect their privacy and do not trespass.